The Changing Face of Gothenburg

Eyassu Gayim

The Changing Face of Gothenburg

Eyassu Gayim

2024 Third edition, Eyassu Gayim ISBN: 978-1-917238-10-6

First edition, printed in Gothenburg, Sweden, by Majornas Grafiska A.B., 2023

Second edition, printed in Gothenburg, Sweden, by Majornas Grafiska A.B., 2023

For feedback and questions concerning this publication send your emails to the author at:

egayim@gmail.com

Domain used by the author for pictures

Picturesbyeyassu.info

Key words

Gothenburg, Gothenburg 400, Gothenburg seasons, Göteborg, Eyassu Gayim and Swedish cities

Dedication

In memory of Mr. John G. Hagman (1925-2022), who welcomed me to Faribault Senior High School (USA) and to his family, when I was an exchange student from Ethiopia in 1966-67. This was only three years after the late Rev. Martin Luther King told Americans about his hopes and dreams. By considering me as a member of his family, Mr. Hagman showed his community how Martin Luther King's dream can be achieved in the real world. I am deeply grateful for the kindness, love and friendship of Mr. Hagman and his family over the past five decades or so.

.

Table of content

Preface

Gothenburg does not brag about being the most important or glamorous city of Sweden, as the capital, Stockholm, does. It is content with its rank as the second largest city in the nation and the fifth largest in the Nordic countries. Historically, the city's proximity to the Swedish, Danish, and Norwegian capitals helped it to develop a dynamic economy based on fishing, shipping, and the automobile industry. For many years, revenues from the export of Volvo cars, which are manufactured in Gothenburg, were mainstay of the Swedish economy, generating significant employment opportunities down the supply chain. The story goes that every time the government was blamed for collecting insufficient taxes from Volvo, the latter would rush to its defence by reminding critics that "If things go badly for Volvo, it will be bad for Sweden".

Gothenburg has earned the reputation of being clean, green, and friendly. As Will Coldwell stated in the Guardian, on 22 February 2017, it was even acknowledged as "the world's most sociable city". It's vibrant social life is rooted in the working-class culture which was developed historically and the long interaction with its Danish and Norwegian neighbours and traders and visitors from West European nations. Tourists are drawn here by its historical sites, museums, and the attractive parks, especially the century-old Liseberg amusement park, the Botanical Garden, and the 137-hectare Castle Forest (Slottsskogen), which hosts a three-day musical festival every August. Gothenburg's long avenues provide an impressive architectural setting for its vibrant shops, restaurants, and cafés in the daytime. The city's nightlight venues illuminate the evenings. It is easy to get around the city using the bus and tram network, soon to be complemented by a new subway system, while in the summer ferries and cruise boats provide additional sightseeing opportunities for tourists.

While cataloguing the attractions of Gothenburg would tempt any visitor, what this author found irresistible was to capture the effects of the seasonal change on the environment. This is why he named this book "The Changing Face of Gothenburg". The book was first published in Gothenburg as the city was celebrating its 400th anniversary, i.e., to wish the residents happy anniversary. Encouraged by the feedback, which was given to the earlier prints, this third edition was prepared by improving the design and changing pictures including for the cover page.

Eyassu Gayim, Gothenburg, 16 February 2024.

Coastal views of the city

Pic #1 Stora Badhusgatan from Göta älv

Pic #2 Lindholmen from Göta älv

Pic #3 Lindholmen from Göta älv

Pic #4 Lilla Bomen from Göta älv

Coastal views of the city

Pic #5 Masthugget's residential quarter

Pic #6 Stora Badhusgatan from Göta älv

Pic #7 Stenpieren from Göta älv

Pic #8 Masthugget's shore from Göta älv

Canal views of the city

Pic #9 Cruising along Norra Hamngatan

Pic #10 Boat peddling along Stora Nygatan

Pic #11 Canal view of Västra Hamngatan 1

Pic #12 Canal view of Norra Hamngatan

Canal views of the city

Pic #13 The Big Habour Canal

Pic #14 The canal, Stampgatan & Slussgatan

Pic #15 Kungsportplatsen from the canal

Pic #16 Stora Nygatan from the canal

Colourful highrise

Pic #17 The high-rise of Gårda: Citygate

Pic #18 Clarion Hotel Draken, Järntorget

Pic #19 The weaver, Hotel

Pic #20 The high-rise of Lilla Bomen

Colourful highrise

Pic #21 Gotha Towers, Korsvägen

Pic #22 Gårda Vesta, office block

Pic #23 Gamlestadstorget

Pic #24 Klaratornet: tallest building in Norden

Gothenburg Churches

Pic #25 Oscar Fredrik Kyrkan

Pic #26 Domkyrkan

Pic #27 Hagakyrkan

Pic #28 Vasakyrkan

Gothenburg Churches

Pic #29 Sankt Johanneskyrkan

Pic #30 Annedalskyrkan

Pic #31 Christinae (German) Church

Pic #32 Masthuggetskyrkan

Summer tourist activity centers

Pic #33 Skansen Lejonet

Pic #34 Skansen

Pic #35 Liseberg

Pic # 36 Trädgårdsföreningen's park entrance

Summer street views

Pic #37 Olskrokstorget

Pic #38 Grönsakstorget

Pic #39 Frölunda Torg

Pic #40 Lindholmenspiren

Summer street views

Pic #41 Drottningstorget

Pic #42 Kungstorget

Pic #43 Gustav Adolfs Torg

Pic #44 Järntorget

Summer street views

Pic #45 Götaplatsen

Pic #46 Kungsportsavenyen

Pic #47 Östra Larmgatan

Pic #48 Haga

Summer street views

Pic #49 Linneagatan

Pic #50 Värmlandsgatan

Pic #51 Kungsgatan

Pic #52 Vasagatan

Colourful buildings

Pic #53 Våghuset, Järntorget

Pic #54 Västra Frölunda residential area

Pic #55 Residential area, Gamlestadstorget

Pic #56 Gårda's high-rise

Misty autumn days

Pic #57 Fog overtaking Klaratornet

Pic #58 Misty day in Stampgatan's kyrkogård

Pic #59 Misty day around Christinae Church

Pic #60 Misty day on the coast of Göta älv

Wet and windy autumn days

Pic #61 Windy day in Östra kyrkogård

Pic #62 Storm in Hjalmar Brantingsplatsen

Pic #63 Rainy day in Olskroken

Pic #64 Rainbow in Olskroken

Colourful autumn days

Pic #65 Vasagatan in the autumn

Pic #66 Stampgatan

Pic #67 Gamla Allé in the autumn

Pic #68 Olkskrostorget in the autumn

Colourful autumn days

Pic #69 Slussgatan in the autumn

Pic #70 king's park in the autumn

Pic #71 Trädgårdsföreningen's entrance, autumn

Pic #72 Gothenburg University, Vasagatan 1

Winter days, - snowfall

Pic #73 Snowfall in Olkskroken

Pic #74 Snowfall around Stockholmsgatan

Pic #75 Parked cars after the snow storm

Pic #76 Christmas in Stampgatan kyrkogård

Winter scenes

Pic #77 Kungsportsavenyen in the winter

Pic #78 Truck (caterpillar) on the fronzen canal

Pic #79 Brunnsparken in the winter

Pic #80 Winter in Trädgårdsföreningenspark

Winter scenes

Pic #81 Kungsportsplatsen in the winter

Pic #82 Kungstorget in the winter

Pic #83 Östra Larmgatan in the winter

Pic #84 Prinsgatan: Skansen from a distance

Winter scenes

Pic #85 Vasagatan in the winter

Pic #86 Linneagatan in the winter

Pic #87 Central Station in the winter

Pic #88 Frölunda Torg in the winter

Winter days and the ice

Pic #89 The frozen canal near Kungsportplatsen

Pic #90 Ice skating on the frozen canal

Pic #91 Ice formation around building edges

Pic #92 Ice blocks sliding from water pipes

Winter afternoons

Pic #93 Winter afternoon, Östra Larmgatan

Pic #94 Winter afternoon, Hissinge Bridge

Pic #95 Winter afternoon, Kungsportsaveny

Pic #96 Winter afternoon, Kungsportplaten

Gothenburg's clouds

Pic #97 Cloud nuclear explosion?

Pic #98 Cloud bear?

Pic #99 Portrait of a cloud man?

Pic #100 Cloud pipline?

Gothenburg's clouds

Pic #101 Cloud ribs or stairs?

Pic #102 Cloud spade?

Pic #103 Cloud snake?

Pic #104 Cloud plane descending?

Gothenburg's sunsets

Pic #105 Sunset #1

Pic #106 Sunset #2

Pic #107 Sunset #3

Pic #108 Sunset #4

Pic #109 Sunset #5

Pic #110 Sunset #6

Pic #111 Sunset #7

Pic #112 Sunset # 8

Gothenburg's summer flowers

Pic #113 Gothenburg street flowers

Pic #114 Gothenburg street flowers

Pic #115 Gothenburg street flowers

Pic #116 Gothenburg street flowers

Gothenburg's summer flowers

Pic #117 Gothenburg park flowers

Pic #118 Gothenburg park flowers

Pic #119 Gothenburg park flower

Pic #120 Gothenburg park flowers

Colourful trees

Pic #121 Tree with green leaves

Pic #122 Tree with green & yellow leaves

Pic #123 Tree with green and red leaves

Pic #124 Tree with green & yellow leaves

Colourful trees

Pic #125 Tree with: yellow & golden leaves

Pic #126 Tree with bright yellow leaves

Pic #127 Tree with bright purple leaves

Pic #128 Tree with bright red leaves

The effect of the seasons on one tree

Pic #129 The life-cycle of one tree, June

Pic #130 The life-cycle of one tree, September

Pic #131 The life-cycle of one tree, November

Pic #132 The life-cycle of one tree, March

The effect of seasons on trees

Pic #133 Nya Allé in June

Pic #134 Nya Allé in September

Pic #135 Nya Allé in October

Pic #136 Nya Allé in February

The effect of seasons on trees

Pic #137 Gubberparken in June

Pic #138 Gubberparken in October

Pic #139 Gubberparken in November

Pic #140 Gubberparken in March

About the author and this publication

The author of this publication is a jurist by academic discipline. After working briefly as a bank attorney, he pursued his post-graduate studies in Sweden, France and Norway and subsequently worked as a researcher or teacher for Swedish, Finnish, and American universities. The books and articles which he has authored concern mostly political conflicts or international human rights law. Photography is his hobby. In this area he has contributed three other previous publications, namely, i. "San Diego: Pictures of the Districts Around the Center", ii. "Skyscape: Images of Clouds, the Sky and the Sun", and, iii. "Nature: Pictures of Trees and Small Plants". They were published in 2020 by the University of Gothenburg's Printing Office. Currently, he works as a consultant for Academic Light, an online private business which was established by him in Gothenburg, Sweden.

This publication was first released, in limited copies, in August 2023 when the historical city of Gothenburg was celebrating the four hundred anniversaries of its foundation. Encouraged by the feedback, a second edition was issued by adding pictures. While the main aim in coming up with this third edition is to make the book available for the broader public, using Kindle.com, this opportunity was also seized to update it by introducing more pictures and improving the layouts.